MW00572838

HEALTH CENTER, LLC

**304-422-5600**

Psalm 119:73

# This Diary Belongs To

_____

*How precious are your thoughts about me, O God!*
Psalm 139:17

# The Sister Circle

# A Discovery Diary

## LEARN TO LOVE YOURSELF

CREATED FOR YOU BY:
VONETTE BRIGHT
& NANCY MOSER

*The Sister Circle, A Discovery Diary*
*Learn to Love Yourself*

Published by
New*Life Publications*
A ministry of Campus Crusade for Christ
P.O. Box 620877
Orlando, FL 32862-0877

Sister Circle is a trademark of Tyndale House Publishers, Inc.

Cover Layout by Urick Design, Rick Johnson artwork used by permission from
Tyndale House Publishers, Inc.
Interior Design and type by Urick Design

Printed in Mexico

**Library of Congress Cataloging-in-Publication Data**

Discovery Diary Volume 1/Vonette Bright & Nancy Moser
ISBN 1-56399-200-0

# Dear Sisters,

Here we are. How we got here is one of those great mysteries. We are two women from different roots, different generations, different educational backgrounds and interests, from different parts of the country. It is such a miracle we got together in the first place. The odds were against it. And yet, we did. Through the last two years, we have come to recognize that God had a plan for us. But even beyond the sisterhood we've been blessed to share, we know that we were brought together for *you*, to share with *you*, to talk with *you*, to be sisters with *you*.

Women have a unique capacity to bond. We can bond with the woman in front of us at the checkout line at Wal-Mart, or exchange child-rearing tips with another woman in an elevator. We don't need a formal introduction. We plunge in—and are blessed. Men generally don't do this, and more amazingly, don't seem to *want* to do this (they don't know what they're missing.) This kinship we women feel for each other, and the ability—and desire—to draw other females into our lives, is the key to *The Sister Circle Series* and these companion *Discovery Diaries*.

When women are together we zero in on how we are the same, and yet, we also don't seem to mind how we're different. This applies to the small details of our lives as well as the big things in our lives. For instance, I, Vonette wear bright pinks and teals and I, Nancy prefer rusts and olives. And yet, when we met in Wheaton, Illinois to work on this project we both wore black and white checkered suits. (see the picture) It was totally unplanned, and yet indicative of how we'd come to think alike, seeking a common ground.

That's what we pray will happen to you when you form an actual Sister Circle of your own. You will know some of the women, but some might be strangers. Yet after one get-together, in true sister fashion, you will be strangers-no-more. We're hoping the friendships that start through these Circles, and through the discovery of the faith principles in the books, will last a lifetime. We're merely providing a reason to get together. The rest is up to you.

We pray that God will guide you during your discoveries, and bring you closer to your new sisters-in-Christ—and to Him. For *He* is the real reason we're together. To Him be the glory forever.

Many blessings to all of you, dear sisters.

*Nancy Moser*

*Vonette Z. Bright*

*See how very much our heavenly
Father loves us,
for He allows us to be called His
children,
and we really are!*

1 John 3:1

**Sister Talk** When was the last time you felt giddy about the day ahead? We know it's hard to feel that way about dishes, diapers or day-planners. Our lives become consumed by minute, mundane moments, but it doesn't have to be that way. Believe it or not, these moments are part of a greater plan. A Divine plan. Not that you don't have choices. You do. Yet every moment that you want to be different can be different. There is no magic formula, or how-to list, but there is an intriguing, freeing process you can use to find out who you are and why you are so extremely special. There is a way to discover your Life Imprint, and we will discuss this concept later on.

So how do you do this? One way to begin is to pinpoint the unique way God has made you. We are all well aware that each of us is different. We have distinct personalities, temperaments, talents, weaknesses, and gifts that affect the way we think and handle every situation. Some are brought about by our environment, but some are innate—born into us, designed in us by our Creator. This is not a random thing. If you get nothing else out of this diary, get this: God has made you a unique individual because He loves *you* and has a unique plan for *your* life. The challenge is to find out *how* you're unique, *why* you should love yourself as He loves you, and *what* that plan is.

Much has been said about self-esteem, self-worth, and self-love. Unfortunately, most of what we have heard has led us to believe that who we are and how we act is a result of the influence of other people and things outside of our control. This has also resulted in a lack of recognition of who we are in Christ Jesus. As women of faith we must accept God's love and in turn, love ourselves

*You watched me as I was being formed in utter seclusion,*
*as I was woven together in the dark of the womb.*
*You saw me before I was born.*
*Every day of my life was recorded in your book.*
*Every moment was laid out*
*before a single day had passed.*

*How precious are your thoughts about me,*
*O God!*
*They are innumerable!*
*I can't even count them;*
*they outnumber the grains of sand!*

*And when I wake up in the morning,*
*you are still with me!*
*Psalm 139: 15 - 18*

The joy and freedom that comes with being able to confess that you care about yourself, that you are worthy of God's love, that you are commanded by Him to love yourself, will change your life.

Every woman is a unique creation designed with a specific purpose. You were not born and *then* God decided what you should do. The character of God would not allow for you to come into this world without a specific plan.

*Before you were born I set you apart.*
*Jeremiah 1: 5*

To live effectively, God has provided each of us with talents, abilities, desires, motivations, wishes, dreams, thoughts, passions . . . and has equipped us with gifts, traits, and qualities to achieve His plan.

## Self Portrait

You may approach this first *Discovery Diary* with a bit of curiosity. Give it a go and we think you will find your own insight so revealing and encouraging that you will look forward to the time spent getting to know yourself better. What have you got to lose?

Your *Discovery Diary* is not a how-to or what-to-do book. It has been prayerfully crafted to provide you a way to discover your unique potential that everyday life may have partially overshadowed.

Facing a blank page in a journal may be natural to some, motivating to others, and horribly frightening to the rest of you. Even the idea of recording thoughts *can* be intimidating. But this is not "true confession" time. The One who made you knows your weaknesses. We want you to discover your strengths. This *Discovery Diary* is a positive self-portrait: *Everything You've Ever Wanted to Know About You, But Were Afraid to Ask.* Hey, we're asking!

We have sectioned the Diary, not by calendar days, but by *Impressions.* Each Impression has multiple parts. One part is where we talk to you in our *Sister Talk,* not as if we have all the answers (but we *do* know the One who does!) but because, as women, we are in this together and we have feelings similar to yours. Short of being in your home with you, these *Sister Talk* chats are our way of reaching out to you, hopefully to open your heart and mind to reveal the true value of *you.*

Within these chats and the *Impressions,* we will give you an opportunity for self-discovery. This is a place where you'll get a chance to think (and write) about your own life. This is your personal chat with yourself (my, aren't you good company?) These sections are called **My Discovery** and hopefully you will have plenty of space to write.

Through it all, we will refer to *The Sister Circle* novel, including excerpts that will help illustrate the life-issues highlighted in the Diary.

Now, for the fun part . . .

# Time Together

Face it. We each have days when we don't like ourselves. There's something refreshing about knowing that other women think the same thoughts, feel the same feelings, experience similar frustrations and self-doubt. Having time together with other women is a lost luxury. Everything and every-one has an agenda. It's going to a home-party where you feel obligated to buy something. It's the school meeting that drags on. It's the Sunday school class when the teacher didn't prepare. These activities drain us. Do you ever long for quality time with girlfriends? Remember those carefree days as a teenager when you could talk nonsense and it somehow seemed world changing? Giggles would fill the room to the ceiling and bounce back again, and the most significant problem you had was a pimple appearing before a big date.

What happened when we grew up? What happened when we went to college, married, and had babies? The carefree sense of freedom—freedom from financial and family responsibilities—vanished. But we *can* feel free. Our freedom needs to be centered in being everything God designed us to be: free to be you; free to be me. Free to be us—together. Why have we isolated ourselves from our girlfriends? We need to laugh and share our experiences. We need each other. That's why we want to encourage you to be a part of a Sister Circle.

Your circle may include just one sister or many. Remember taking the hands of a girlfriend, leaning back and twirling around? The balance you created by holding tightly to each other allowed you to swirl and twirl and not fall down. We need to find that balance in our lives as women. Hold tightly to your sisters and find security as you grow in your walk of faith.

## Explore and Connect

A Sister Circle is not intended to add another meeting to your schedule, nor to be something that expects something from you; that drains you. Our goal is to create an atmosphere of *giving*, enthusiastically encouraging each other, providing women a legitimate reason to get together to celebrate the joy of sisterhood. It's a time for you and your friends to read a book, share some thoughts, and maybe indulge in a comfort food, but most importantly just be together.

What we want to offer you with the *Sister Circle Discovery Diaries* and-or belonging to an actual Sister Circle, is an opportunity to explore your journey of self-discovery and to connect with other women.

Now that we've totally overwhelmed you . . .

Grab a cup of coffee, sit in a cushy chair, take a deep breath, and repeat after us the Sister Circle pledge:

*Without wavering, I will hold tightly to the hope I say I have,*
*for God can be trusted to keep His promise.*
*I will think of ways to encourage my sisters to outbursts of love and good deeds.*

Hebrews 10: 23-24 (slightly personalized)

## Your Life Imprint

We want you to read three references in the Bible where you will find specific God-given abilities listed.

*God has given each of us the ability to do certain things well. So if God has given you the ability to prophesy, speak* out when you have faith that God is speaking through you. If your gift is that of serving others, serve them well. If you are a teacher, do a good job of teaching. If your gift is to encourage others, do it! If you have money, share it generously. If God has given you leadership ability, take the responsibility seriously. And if you have a gift for showing kindness to others, do it gladly.

Romans 12:6-8

Now there are different kinds of spiritual gifts, but it is the same Holy Spirit who is the source of them all. There are different kinds of service in the church, but it is the same Lord we are serving. There are different ways God works in our lives, but it is the same God who does the work through all of us. A spiritual gift is given to each of us as a means of helping the entire church.

To one person the Spirit gives the ability to give wise advice; to another he gives the gift of special knowledge. The Spirit gives special faith to another, and to someone else he gives the power to heal the sick. He gives one person the power to perform miracles, and to another the ability to prophesy. He gives someone else the ability to know whether it is really the Spirit of God or another spirit that is speaking. Still another person is given the ability to speak in unknown languages, and another is given the ability to interpret what is being said.  It is the one and only Holy Spirit who distributes these gifts. He alone decides which gift each person should have.

1 Corinthians 12:4-11

He is the one who gave these gifts to the church: the apostles, the prophets, the evangelists, and the pastors and teachers.  Their responsibility is to equip God's people to do his work and build up the church, the body of Christ, until we come to such unity in our faith and knowledge of God's Son that we will be mature and full grown in the Lord, measuring up to the full stature of Christ.

Ephesians 4:11-13

After reading these verses, do you identify with any of the God-gifted attributes? If you're not sure, you might ask yourself: what brings me a sense of satisfaction? What do others say I do well? Most likely the enjoyment extends from the fact that you are using your God-given abilities.

It is not our intent to present an exhaustive study of who you are. But your spiritual gift will be evident as you discover your Life Imprint.  And more importantly, you need to remember that the Holy Spirit will empower you to do anything God calls you to do.

In this first *Discovery Diary,* we want to start you on a journey to understanding that the fingerprint of God is imprinted on you, HIS very image. Your Life Imprint is a combination of many factors from genetics, environment, and geography. In this diary we will focus on just two elements of your Life Imprint : spiritual gifts and natural temperament. Future *Discovery Diaries* will explore more aspects of what makes you, you.

Think about Peerbaugh Place. In the novel, *The Sister Circle,* you may have recognized the unique qualities of the characters. Did you relate to the actions and attitudes of a specific woman? Each of the seven females in *The Sister Circle* demonstrate one of the special gifts highlighted in Romans 12.

**Piper The Perceiver:** Piper understands and sees the larger picture. She addresses the spiritual needs of those around her and keeps them centered on spiritual principles.

She is the "eyes" of the body. She sees what's truly going on and doesn't mince words, nor shy away from trying to persuade others to see God at work around them. Though she sees sin in others, she also sees it in herself, and even rejoices in identifying her weaknesses, knowing that God will do a good work through her struggles. But because she does recognize her faults, she often has a poor self image, always aware she can be better.

Piper likes to be away from people—for she never considers herself alone. She truly thinks of God as always present and finds companionship in Him. She holds herself to strict standards and desires to be obedient to God at all costs.

*However,* Piper tends to be judgmental and blunt. She is so goal conscious that she forgets to praise others when they have a partial victory. She is pushy and intolerant of opinions that she sees as anti-God.

**Summer the Server:** Summer recognizes the needs of others and is quick to meet them. She is a detail person, with a good memory. She enjoys people and will stay with a task until it is completed. She will do more than she's asked to do, but needs to feel appreciated. She does not want to lead, but would rather do a job herself than let someone else do it. She dislikes clutter.

Summer is the "hands" of the body; the worker who serves, addressing the practical needs of others.

Summer has a hard time saying no and often ignores her own needs in order to fill the needs of others. She isn't good with words, but shows she cares through action.

*However,* Summer doesn't understand when other people don't want to help and can also become pushy by being too eager to help herself. She also finds it hard to let other people serve her and is easily hurt when unappreciated.

**Tessa the Teacher:** Tessa likes things to be logical and based on truth. Facts are very important to her and she loves to study and do research. She enjoys word studies and is skeptical of anything taken out of context. She is smart, sharp, and self-disciplined. She tries to keep her emotions under control and only has a select circle of friends. She has very strong convictions.

Tessa is the "mind" of the body, challenging the intellect of others, keeping them studying and learning.

*However,* Tessa gets so caught up in facts that she neglects the practical life application of the truth. She doesn't like listening to other opinions and tends to be prideful about her own expertise and intelligence. She is legalistic and can often get sidetracked by new projects that perk her interest.

**Mae the Motivator:** Mae loves life. She loves people and lives to encourage them to be all they can be. She is a hands-on person, preferring to experience something rather than reading about it. She is a good talker and a good listener who needs the give and take of a responsive audience. She doesn't judge others harshly but is accepting because she wants to help people be all they can be. She makes decisions easily and completes what she starts. She has lots of friends because she makes people feel good about themselves. She expects a lot of others, and of herself.

Mae is the "mouth" of the body, sharing truth, nourishing the psychological side of her friends.

*However,* in her eagerness, Mae tends to interrupt to give her opinions or advice. She tends to have a cut-and-dried answer for everything and can be overly confident. Plus, if someone doesn't make an effort to change a problem in their lives, she becomes perturbed and washes her hands of them.

***Audra the Administrator:*** Organization is key to Audra's life. She's good at communicating and expressing her ideas. She's a leader with a broad perspective on things. She can get people to act, giving them a logical way to respond to a problem or task. Her enthusiasm comes from getting things done in the best, most efficient way possible. She respects authority, and doesn't necessarily need to get credit for her work, as long she feels her own satisfaction in the process. She is a list-maker and a note writer. She likes to be challenged and doesn't thrive on routine.

Audra is the "shoulders" of the body, taking on the responsibility others often don't want to assume. She takes care of functional needs, keeping others organized as she increases their vision.

*However,* Audra becomes upset when others don't see her vision toward a goal, or don't work hard. She can be a perfectionist, expecting a lot from herself and others. The "goal" is the thing, and this focus can often make her hard to deal with as she neglects the people involved in achieving that goal.

***Evelyn the Empathizer:*** Evelyn has a great capacity to love. She always looks for the good in people and is attracted to people who need her. She wants everyone to get along and takes great pains not to offend. She is trusting and trustworthy, but avoids conflicts and confrontations. She is thoughtful of others. She is ruled by the heart rather than the head. She is cheerful and feels what others feel. She is a crusader for good causes.

Evelyn is the "heart" of the body, addressing the emotional needs of others. She feels for us and with us.

*However,* Evelyn is indecisive and easily hurt. Sometimes she empathizes too much with others' hurts, and feels them herself. She is often soft to the point of being wishy-washy. It's hard for her to take a stand.

***Gillie the Giver:*** Gillie gives freely of money, possessions, time, energy, and love. She gives the best and gives toward a specific need. She is quick to volunteer. She is good at business and understands how to give wisely, being a good steward of her resources. She realizes God is the Source of her financial supply and so feels special joy in giving.

Gillie is the "arms" of the body. She extends them to give to others, making sure their material needs are met.

*However,* she tends to pressure others to give and often wants control over how her gifts are used. She also can use financial giving as a way to get out of other responsibilities.

**D**My**iscovery** At this point in my journey, which one of the characters—and their spiritual gift—do I identify with most?

_____

_____

_____

_____

_____

In what specific way?

_____

_____

_____

_____

_____

_____

_____

_____

Let's go a step further, and move from spiritual gifts to personality types. You may be familiar with personality profiles or various forms of testing designed to define how you behave. Most likely you are a combination of many types as God equips you to meet the demands of your circumstances. However, on a day-to-day basis the characteristics of one personality type tends to dominate. These characteristics influence everything we do—

- How we communicate
- How we learn
- How we parent
- How we dress
- How we shop
- How we eat
- How we decorate
- How we share our faith
- How we worship

To help you remember your personality type, we have related each of the characters to an element of God's marvelous creation (we admit having a lot of fun doing this.)

Try to identify which character goes with each element:

**Wind** - is often hot, aggressive, intolerant, and powerful. It takes over; its goal is to grow stronger. It blows over people and can be intrusive. Yet it can also be refreshing.

**Earth** - is non-confrontational, nourishing, constant, and peaceful. It conforms to whatever is happening around it.

**Sky** - surrounds us, never touching, and unable to be touched. It's unpredictable, moody, expansive, and giving, spreading its wealth from horizon to horizon.

**Water** - envelops us and can be calm or churning, refreshing or dangerous. It's fascinating and yet relentless. It both purifies and tarnishes. It can carry us, we can cross through it, go under it, or float on top of it. It spurs us toward change.

**Plants** - are dependable. They come up the same time every year. The seeds bring forth their own kind of plant. An oak is not a daisy. They are ordered, controlled, capable, and are affected by where they are put to grow. They are at their best when pruned, yet can go wild. Plants flourish when they are in the right conditions, place, and season.

**Snow** - is unique, peaceful, intricate, quiet, fragile, and blankets the world. It purifies, provides nourishment, and joy. Yet it can be cold and destructive if there is too much of it.

**Sunshine** - awakens and stimulates, delights, yet can burn. It's mood altering. It lights up everything in its path with clarity and warmth.

**My Discovery** Which one of these elements of God's creation do I identify with?

_____

_____

_____

_____

_____

_____

_____

_____

_____

_____

_____

_____

In what specific ways?

_____

_____

_____

_____

_____

_____

_____

_____

_____

_____

_____

_____

_____

_____

_____

_____

_____

_____

_____

Now, you have a starting point. So let's delve into your self-discovery. Ready?

impression one
# Independence

*On the whole, God's love for us is a much safer subject to think about than our love for him.*
C.S. Lewis

*The Sister Circle:* Chapter 12, page 302

Mae had tried to go back to sleep after Summer's mishap but had only managed to lay in bed, very much awake. Everyone else was with their respective families, celebrating Mother's Day.

But it was just another day for her.

She couldn't remember the last time she'd gotten any special attention on Mother's Day. Five years ago? Ten?

*And whose fault is that?*

Mae flipped to her other side and pulled a pillow to her chest. She'd brought up her children to be independent beings. Was there anything wrong with that?

*Independence doesn't have to negate closeness.* The relationships between the women of Peerbaugh Place proved that. They led lives independent of each other, yet bound by . . . bound by . . .

Love.

The greatest love is shown when people lay down their lives for their friends.

Mae subjected her pillow to a strangle-hold. She loved her children. But did they love her?

*If they loved me they'd call me on Mother's Day. They'd send me a card, they'd—They can't send me a card if they don't know where I live. What was the last address I shared with them?*

Mae tried to remember. Her children didn't know about Peerbaugh Place nor the apartment before that. But she did remember getting a card from Ringo when she lived in that bizarre little apartment over the pizzeria. It had taken Mae a good year to tolerate Italian food after that, the smell of marinara permeating her every breath. But it had been even longer ago since she'd talked with Starr. Last she'd heard, Ringo was a roadie with a rock band and Starr was working for some publishing house. Neither was married, though last she'd known, Starr was living with some broker-type. Her children had their lives and she had hers. Wasn't a parent supposed to bring up kids so they could butter their own slice in this world?

*But that doesn't mean you shouldn't have contact with each other.*

It was a two-way street. They could try to get in touch with her. They could—

They couldn't. Not if they didn't have her address or her phone number. Her self-imposed freedom, instead of offering wide open vistas, suddenly seemed very closed—with very high walls.

A prison of loneliness.

Mae pulled the covers over her head.

**Sister Talk**   Denial shows itself in many ways. Mae was arguing with herself. She was in denial. She was an independent woman who reared independent children. It never bothered her before. Why now?

Sometimes we accidentally discover the imbalance in our lives by watching others. It's important that we accept these moments of realization as positive guidance—even when we don't like what we see.

**My Discovery**   Have I ever seen my faults through someone else's actions?

_____

_____

_____

_____

_____

_____

_____

"Sisters together are a force to be reckoned with."

Karen Brown

_____
_____
_____
_____
_____
_____
_____
_____
_____
_____
_____

Was I prompted to change or ignore the issue?

_____
_____
_____

Proverbs 27:9

The heartfelt
counsel of
a friend is
as sweet as
perfume and
incense.

_____
_____
_____
_____
_____
_____
_____
_____

_____

_____

_____

_____

_____

_____

**Sister Talk** Mae, the **Water/Motivator** individual flows freely over everything and everyone in its path. A healthy level of independence can be difficult for the **Water/Motivator** to achieve. In your zeal to motivate you may appear arrogant and insensitive. However, on the flip side, it's your healthy sense of independence that allows you to be used by God to inspire others.

As sisters, we can admit to each other that our independence is not nearly so rewarding as relying on each other—being dependent. Isn't it satisfying to delight in your sister's new hairdo, her promotion, or the fact that she opted for an apple over cheesecake when you went out for lunch (and didn't say a thing when _you_ ordered french fries.) Yet understand, you may not feel the same about everyone. The key is to find the balance between bonding and obligation; between friendships that are a blessing rather than a burden. That kind of freedom is sisterhood at its best.

# My Discovery

Is my independence keeping me from having a good relationship with someone? Who? Why? What action can I take to remedy the situation?

_____

_____

_____

_____

_____

_____

_____

_____

# Sister Talk

You don't have to be wise to understand the need for relationships. The lack of a meaningful relationship made Mae realize she was missing something. We need our family, we need our friends, but we need even more. In order to be complete and feel whole, we need to develop an ultimate dependence on God. Once we accept that need, every relationship benefits.

If God knows how many hairs are on your head and every time a sparrow falls (Matthew 10: 29-31) then how can you doubt He cares about the details of your life? If it's important to you, it's important to Him.

# D My iscovery

What small detail am I trying to handle on my own that I should handle with God's help?

_____
_____
_____
_____
_____
_____
_____
_____
_____
_____
_____
_____
_____
_____
_____
_____

What big issue am I trying to handle on my own that I should handle with God's help?

_____
_____
_____

> With sisters,
> the only
> strings
> attached are
> from the
> heart.

_____
_____
_____
_____
_____
_____
_____
_____
_____
_____
_____
_____
_____
_____
_____
_____
_____
_____

**Sister Talk** Nancy here: I'll share one big lesson I've learned that is put to the test during arguments with my spouse. We used to both give as good as we got, and the argument intensified and got us no where. But one time, during a moment of clarity in the middle of the battle, I decided to turn to God—to depend on Him and not myself—and found myself praying: "Lord, help me not say anything you don't approve of." I expected God to answer

34

such a prayer by giving me the exact words I needed to really *get* my husband and win the argument. But you know what words He told me to say? No words. Nada. Nothing. God gave me the strength to depend on His words instead of my own, even when that meant being silent (how dare He!). Without my words to fuel the battle-flame, the argument soon died. And that, in itself, was a victory of dependence upon God.

## His Imprint

There is no honor in being independent. Solomon, the wisest man ever, wrote this: "If you listen to constructive criticism, you will be at home among the wise. If you reject criticism, you only harm yourself; but if you listen to correction, you grow in understanding. Fear of the LORD teaches a person to be wise; humility precedes honor" (Proverbs 15: 31-33).

The first line in Rick Warren's wonderful book, *The Purpose Driven Life*, is "It's not about you." Ever since reading that line, those four words have sat on my shoulder, jumping up and down to get my attention at key moments when independence and self-absorption threaten. No indeed, it's not about us.

It's about Him. Don't forget it.

*True sisters appreciate their differences as much as their similarites.*

impression two
# Perfectionism

*"The (woman) who aims at perfection
in everything achieves it in nothing."*
Delacroix

*The Sister Circle:* Chapter 9, page 218

"I tried putting [Summer] in your room," [Evelyn said,] "but she didn't want to muss the covers. I didn't think you'd mind, but she was adamant."

Audra took a deep breath, finding calm. Why couldn't she ease up on her need for order? How many times had her own mother chastised her, saying, "Audra, she's just a little girl." Audra knew what she *should* do, but found it incredibly hard to do it.

"Audra, if you want, call me later."

Audra's guilt rode her shoulders like a burdened pack. "I'm sorry you have to handle all this, Evelyn. And I'm sorry...she could've slept in our room." It sounded as lame as it was.

"I know that. But be assured, she's doing fine here with Aunt Evelyn. Truly."

Audra said her good-byes and went back to work, fighting a twinge of an emotion she had a hard time defining. And then it hit her like a two-by-four across the back of the legs, and she felt herself buckle at the knowledge.

37

Summer *was* doing fine at home, snug in Aunt Evelyn's bed.

Better off there than with her mother?

**Sister Talk** Plant/Administrators thrive on structure, on conditions being right. Preparation and follow-through are essential for survival. If this is you, you're a bit high maintenance, and you focus on details. This can be a good thing: the world can use more organization. Or a bad thing, as you struggle with an overprotective tendency or use your organizational talents to complicate situations.

For Christian women, the subtle pressure to be perfect can be damaging. Women today have professional opportunities that can become very demanding of their physical and mental energy. The tension in balancing the role of wife, lover, mother, and friend with career goals, financial expectations . . . Add to this our culture's obsession with physical beauty and the price tag is beyond our emotional budget. We can't handle it.

Sometimes, as an escape mechanism, a woman focuses on one dimension of her life with such intense scrutiny and perfectionism that she sets up herself—and others—for failure. There's just no way such perfection can be attained— or maintained.

The obsessive pursuit of perfectionism is destructive and the amount of time the perfectionist wastes out of her life is a sin. Yet, on the flip side, the desire to be perfect—like Christ—is an ongoing healthy quest and process. The hard part is finding the balance.

$D$iscovery My One area in my life that takes an inordinate amount of time and attention is:

_____

_____

_____

_____

_____

_____

Have I ever missed an activity because my house wasn't in order, or my personal appearance didn't suit me?

_____

_____

_____

_____

_____

_____

Am I willing to risk asking my family if
I've been too demanding in any one area?

_____

_____

_____

_____

_____

_____

What they said:

_____

_____

_____

_____

_____

_____

_____

_____

_____

_____

_____

_____

In what area is it possible for me to change?

_____
_____
_____
_____
_____
_____
_____
_____
_____
_____
_____
_____
_____
_____
_____
_____
_____
_____

**Sister Talk** We hope you haven't been too hard on yourself, because there is a perfect place for the pursuit of excellence in a woman's life. Just don't overdo—in either direction.

*"Oh, don't worry; I wouldn't dare say that I am as wonderful as these other men who tell you how important they are!*

*But they are only comparing themselves with each other, and measuring themselves by themselves. What foolishness!"*

Review the list below contrasting Perfectionism with Excellence:

| Perfectionism | Pursuit Of Excellence |
|---|---|
| An idealist | A realist |
| Fears failure | Accepts failure as a part of life |
| Defensive about criticism | Profits from criticism |
| Dwells on mistakes | Learns from mistakes |
| Demands success | Desires success |
| "My best isn't good enough" | "I'm pleased with my best" |
| "I hate to lose and God doesn't like losers." | "I hate to lose, but God loves me, win or lose." |

**D**<sup>My</sup>iscovery Which column did I score highest in? Perfectionism or Excellence? How can I change for the better?

_____

_____

_____

_____

_____

_____

_____

$D^{My}_{iscovery}$ How can my sisters help me pursue excellence?

_____

_____

_____

_____

_____

_____

_____

_____

_____

## His Imprint

The control brought about by perfectionism is not an unnatural desire. But, it is unrealistic. Ease up. Back off. Self-control is a good thing. But God-control is even better. Let Him do it for you. Once you make the conscious decision to let God work in your life, He eagerly jumps in. He's just been waiting for you to say yes!

*"Knowing God leads to self-control. Self-control leads to patient endurance, and patient endurance leads to godliness.*
*Godliness leads to love for other Christians, and finally you will grow to have genuine love for everyone."*

2 Peter 1: 6-7

# impression three
## Solitude

> "Loneliness
> is the
> poverty of
> self. Solitude
> is the
> richness of
> self."
>
> Unknown

> "Loneliness is the first thing which
> God's eye named not good."
> *John Milton*

*The Sister Circle:* Chapter 1, page 3

The silence became a vacuum that sucked away all her energy. She let the solidity of the door guide her as she slid to the floor. Her challis skirt got hung up on a knee, revealing her slip. She moved to pull it primly down, but when she realized there was no one around to see, let it be. That would take getting used to, having no one around.

The tears began to flow uncontrollably—sobs she never expected. Thoughts of her life began to unfold like a book being opened... . She'd lived a pleasant, respectable life, enjoyed good friends, and reared an independent son. Now, in her golden years, was this all she had to show? This was it? Decades of humdrum, monotonous existence coupled with financial struggle?

She sniffed loudly and used her skirt to wipe her face. Then, without warning, she spoke aloud, "God, if You're out there...help! Tell me what I'm supposed to do next."

With effort, she took a deep breath, but the air entered in ragged pieces. Why did she feel so worn out? She used to be full

45

*Stay away from the love of money; be satisfied with what you have. For God has said,*

*"I will never fail you.*

*I will never forsake you."*

of energy, and yet now, as a widow, her strength vacillated between the frenzy of a worker ant and a bug squashed beneath someone's foot. As if sensing her mood, Peppers nudged her face into Evelyn's calf. Evelyn picked her up and let the calico find her favorite position on Evelyn's shoulder, like a baby going to be burped. Peppers' purring resonated against Evelyn's chest like the comforting sound of cicadas on a summer evening.

## Sister Talk

Surveys reveal that loneliness is a very important issue in a woman's life; one she may not recognize. It's important not to internalize or create something that doesn't exist, but . . . have you ever been standing in a busy airport terminal, people brushing by you on every side, and suddenly your mind and heart are flooded with the feeling that you are all alone, separate from the rest of the world? That's loneliness.

The one common ingredient to our lonely feeling is a lack of contact in a relationship. Loneliness has nothing to do with the number of people around you, but is the lack of soul bonding to soul, mind bonding to mind, emotion bonding to emotion.

# $D^{My}_{iscovery}$

Identify the last time I was truly lonely.

_____
_____
_____
_____
_____
_____
_____
_____
_____
_____
_____
_____
_____
_____
_____
_____
_____
_____
_____

1 Peter 1:6

So be truly glad! There is wonderful joy ahead, even though it is necessary for you to endure many trials for a while.

"For the mountains may depart and the hills disappear, but even then I will remain loyal to you. My covenant of blessing will never be broken," says the LORD, who has mercy on you.

**Sister Talk** So we've identified a time when we've been lonely. Now what? Loneliness doesn't need to overwhelm us. With God's help we can learn to deal with loneliness, and put it in proper perspective as a mood and not a permanent state of mind. Recognize it, deal with it, accept it as a normal part of life. If you are working at home, walk outside and take a few deep breaths of fresh air or take a walk with a friend. In a busy place, make eye contact with one person and strike up a conversation. Even a few moments of chit-chat can take our loneliness outside ourselves where it can dissipate. Do an act of kindness for someone to take your mind off yourself.

**My Discovery** What affects my mood?

____ a person?
____ a place?
____ a song?
____ a smell?
____ (what else?)

_____

_____

_____

_____

_____

_____

What can bring about the most dramatic change in my mood?

____ Lighting?
____ Temperature?
____ Physical activity?
____ Food?
____ (what else?)

_____

_____

_____

_____

_____

**Sister talk** Evelyn's loneliness had a season. Being alone is not necessarily being lonely. There is sanity in solitude. Being alone with quiet thoughts, creative ideas, meditative moments, can keep us sane. Sometimes we're too quick to try to get rid of the loneliness, to try to fill the vacuum, when God might be trying to use those moments to speak to us.

And yet we *can* learn to set aside self-pity and *choose* contentment.

*The Sister Circle:* Chapter 10, Page 263

There was one cookie left and Piper eyed it, as did Gillie. They giggled at the

Deuteronomy 33:27

The eternal God is your refuge, and His everlasting arms are under you. He thrusts out the enemy before you; it is He who cries, "Destroy them!"

49

realization. Then Piper picked it up and broke it in two, handing one half to her new friend.

Gillie popped it in her mouth. "Why does it feel like we've just taken a blood oath by sharing the last cookie?"

It was an apt analogy. "The blood oath of two sisters, achieved through chocolate. Much less messy and painful than the manly man method."

Gillie licked her fingers loudly. "Amen to that." She leaned back on the couch and patted her stomach. "It's been wonderful to vent with you, Piper. Two single women trying to make their way in a couples world. I feel like I have a compatriot now."

"You do." Piper stacked the bowls. "To tell you the truth, I was feeling a bit sorry for myself before you came. Although I like being alone, sometimes it gets to me."

"As it does to me." Gillie got up and took the dishes to the kitchen. Piper followed, enjoying the fact that Gillie felt enough at home to move about her apartment freely. "You know what's wonderful about tonight?"

Piper put the dishes in the dishwasher. "The fact we found someone else who knows how to binge at our level?"

"Beyond that—and to say anything is beyond chocolate is quite a feat." She leaned against the counter. "By becoming closer to you, I feel as if I've purchased another insurance policy against loneliness. Not that I'm going to dump myself on your doorstep daily or pepper you with obsessive phone calls." Gillie put a hand to her chest. "And maybe I'm speaking out of turn here, making too much of—"

"No, no," Piper said. "I feel the same way. It's wonderful having another friend to turn to."

"You can't have too many friends."

"Indeed, you can't." Piper felt a satisfaction that went way beyond chocolate.

*D*My*iscovery* Do I think Gillie and Piper are content?

_____

_____

_____

_____

_____

_____

_____

_____

_____

_____

_____

How does their alone-ness differ from Evelyn's?

_____

_____

_____

_____

_____

_____

_____

_____

_____

_____

**Sister Talk** People like Gillie give, but whether or not the **Sky/Giver** is appreciated, a sense of loneliness can surface if they believe their worth is attached to the value of their gift rather than *their* value as a person. This can make them feel very lonely.

Take solace in remembering the ultimate Giver of all time. Jesus gave *everything*, yet suffered horrible rejection. Few appreciated His sacrifice. Yet through His gracious nature, He rejoices each and every time that a soul accepts His gift. Learn from Him.

**D**$^{My}_{iscovery}$ I am alerted to the fact that it's time to move away from my busyness in order to grab some solitude when:

_____
_____
_____
_____
_____
_____
_____
_____
_____
_____
_____

I find precious solitude in:

_____
_____
_____
_____
_____
_____
_____

_____

_____

_____

_____

_____

**Sister Talk** Sometimes just stopping what you're doing, closing your eyes, and taking a deep breath can let you glimpse a moment of rejuvenating solitude.

*The LORD is my shepherd;*
*I have everything I need.*
*He lets me rest in green meadows;*
*he leads me beside peaceful streams.*
*He renews my strength.*

*Psalm 23: 1-3*

How do we hold onto such a moment? We can't stop living and be held in suspension; we have to get on with our daily lives.

When our hearts and minds are reconciled to our Creator there is an inner solitude to draw from, one that's based and rooted in Him. It's not something we can do or say, or a place we are, but a state of being. In the midst of a hurried, hectic life, we can find a peace that passes understanding.

*I am leaving you with a gift
peace of mind and heart.
And the peace I give isn't like the
peace the world gives,
so don't be troubled or afraid.*

John 14: 27

# D My iscovery   How can I help a lonely sister?

_____

_____

_____

_____

_____

_____

## His Imprint

Where did Jesus go to recharge? He didn't seek out the crowds, nor stop living, but when He could, He withdrew into solitude. But he was never alone. God is with us in every circumstance, in every moment, in any mood. He can be the Savior in our solitude. In fact, He instructs us to be still. Stop fighting it. Be still. And know Him.

*Be still, and know that I am God.*
Psalm 46: 10 (NIV)

impression four
# Courage
and
# Confidence

> *"I wouldn't trust the greatest man in the world with the wrong woman.."*
> Henrietta Mears

> *"No man in the world has more courage than the man who can stop after eating one peanut."*
> Channing Pollock

*The Sister Circle:* Chapter 1, page 10

"Renters. I'll take in boarders!"

Russell shook his head. "Strangers in your house? I don't think that's a good idea."

"I would interview them, screen them. And once they moved in, they wouldn't *be* strangers."

Russell laughed. "You got that right"...

... Evelyn stood and began to pace. Her hands danced as her thoughts pummeled her brain . . . "I've changed." She wasn't sure that was true. *If only Aaron were here. He'd take this idea and run with it.*

"How much rent could you charge?"

Evelyn stopped at the kitchen window, pinched a dead leaf off an African violet, and did the mental math. *There's no mortgage ... just utilities and upkeep. And I'll be getting some Social Security . . .*

"Mom? How much would you charge?"

"I don't know yet. But I'll figure it out."

When she turned back to him, he was shaking his head. "Face it, Mom; you're the last person to tackle such a thing. You're the epitome of disorganization. The house is always clean, but if I asked you right now for a picture of Dad, you would draw photos from five different locations. Why, I've seen you hold a receipt in your hand for a full minute, trying to decide which drawer or purse to stuff it in."

Everything he said was true. "I'll be better. I'll work at it."

"And how are you going to manage rent and damage deposits, house repairs, and tenant disputes? If someone yells at you, you'll probably run out to the porch. Or if they came to you with a sob story about not being able to pay the rent, you'll make them a cup of tea and give them a hug before telling them not to worry about it. So then *I'd* end up worrying about it; I'd end up the bad guy. I'm not sure I'm up for that."

"I'll make it work. I will."

He scooted his chair back. "Would you forget the whole thing if I wrote you a check for a few thousand?"

She straightened her shoulders and shook her head vehemently. "A boarding house is the answer; I know it is."

He stared at her, and there was a hint of disgust in his face. But also resignation. And even pride? "You've never come to a decision this fast in your life, Mom. *How* do you know? How?"

It was a good question that didn't have a clear answer. This feeling of certainty was foreign but undeniable. She put a fist to her heart, where her certainty was lodged. "How do I know? I just do."

**Sister Talk** Considering Evelyn's history of buckling, where was she getting that chutzpah? That feeling of certainty?

Life for the Evelyns of the world, the **Earth/Empathizers**, revolve on an axis of concern. The overwhelming desire is to console, to adapt, to conform. But if you allow yourself to be conformed into oblivion, you can suffer scars.

It doesn't have to be that way. Just because you feel things deeply and don't want to rock the boat doesn't mean you don't have vital, important ideas and contributions to make. When you have biblical confirmation—take a stand. Even if you run into a bit of opposition.

And you may.

We all have dreams and goals, but sometimes other people *do* try to hold us back. Perhaps the main reason is that many people are disconcerted by any change in the status quo (and as an **Earth/Empathizer**, you've given them a rock-solid status quo!) The key is not to let them stop you, but to be like Evelyn, and show a little fortitude. If you don't, you need to ask yourself *why* you don't. Is it because it's easier to blame your lack of courage on others, kidding yourself by saying it's their fault for holding you back, not yours for being cowardly? Be courageous and take a stand! Confidence follows courage. Just think

*Ephesians 3:19*

*"May you experience the love of Christ, though it is so great you will never fully understand it. Then you will be filled with the fullness of life and power that comes from God."*

of what the women of Peerbaugh Place would have lost if Evelyn had not been courageous.

**My Discovery** How have I conformed when I should have been strong? What will the world miss if I am too timid to share the wisdom God has given me?

_____

_____

_____

_____

_____

_____

_____

_____

_____

_____

_____

_____

_____

_____

_____

_____

_____

_____

**Sister Talk** Lots of people in the Bible had to be brave, go against the grain, dare to do something gutsy they knew was God's will. Listen to Moses' words to his protégé, Joshua, when he was questioning his own abilities in conquering the people who lived in the Promised Land: "Be strong and courageous! Do not be afraid of them! The LORD your God will go ahead of you. He will neither fail you nor forsake you" (Deuteronomy 31: 5-6).

God went ahead of them then, and He goes ahead of you now! So be fearful? "If God is for us, who can ever be against us?" (Romans 8: 31).

**My Discovery** What makes me afraid? What's holding me back from living out my full potential? What is God's part in making my dreams become reality? What is my part?

_____

_____

_____

_____

_____

_____

_____

_____

_____

_____

_____

_____

_____

_____

_____

_____

_____

**Sister Talk** It's been said that courage is the absence of fear, yet we know a person can be afraid and show tremendous courage. Fear is proof you realize that *you* can't handle a situation. If you react correctly, you will turn to God and allow Him to work through you to accomplish His will. That takes courage.

Showing courage is also evidence of self-esteem. It's an act of loving yourself. Courage, confidence, self-esteem, and loving yourself have often been looked upon negatively in the Christian world. This is wrong! God loves you enough to have sent His Son to die for YOU (not everyone else but you.) Isn't that evidence of your worth? You must be bold! Get out there! He has a unique plan for your life! Just do it!

*So let us come boldly to the throne of our gracious God.
There we will receive his mercy, and we will find grace to help us when we need it.*
Hebrews 4:16

For God has not given us a spirit of fear and timidity, but of power, love, and self-discipline.

Look at that. God wants us to be bold—bold enough to run to Him. Boldness takes courage. It is courage.

# D<sup>My</sup>iscovery What times in my life have I been courageous and gone after something important to me?

_____

_____

_____

_____

_____

_____

_____

_____

_____

_____

_____

_____

_____

63

> "Courage is resistance to fear, mastery of fear—not absence of fear."
>
> Mark Twain

_____
_____
_____
_____
_____
_____
_____
_____
_____
_____

How was I able to do it?

_____
_____
_____
_____
_____
_____
_____
_____
_____
_____
_____
_____
_____
_____
_____

_____
_____
_____
_____
_____
_____
_____
_____
_____

How did it make me feel?

_____
_____
_____
_____
_____
_____
_____
_____
_____
_____
_____
_____

Psalm 57:2

"I cry out to
God Most
High, to God
who will fulfill
his purpose
for me."

_____

_____

_____

_____

_____

_____

_____

How can my sisters help?

_____

_____

Psalm 138:8

"The LORD
will work
out his plans
for my
life—for your
faithful love,
O LORD,
endures
forever.

Don't abandon
me, for you
made me."

# His Imprint

In heaven all things will be made clear. Your life will be made clear. At that time, do you want to risk having God reveal to you all you *could* have done, but *didn't* do? Or do you want to know that you allowed God to use you to your fullest potential? You need to be like Isaiah. When God asked, "Whom should I send as a messenger to my people? Who will go for us?", Isaiah answered, "Lord, I'll go! Send me" (Isaiah 6:8).

Say it: *Lord, I'll go! Send me!* Say yes to God! Unconditionally—before He even asks a question. Then stand back and be amazed . . .

*Now glory be to God! By his mighty power at work within us,*
*he is able to accomplish infinitely more than we would ever dare to ask or hope.*

Ephesians 3: 20

*Look at the nations and be amazed!*
*Watch and be astounded at what I will do!*
*For I am doing something in your own day,*
*something you wouldn't believe even if someone told you about it.*

Habbakkuk 1:5

He said you can do it. He said He'll be with you every step of the way. So it will come to pass.

impression five

# Resolving Conflict

> *"The only cure for the love of power is the power of love."*
> *Sherri McAdam*

**Sister Talk** The quest for power is *the* number one reason for conflict. The nightly news graphically presents each day's newest battle for control—in living color. Countries, cities, neighborhoods, and families. Everybody wants their piece of the power pie. And everyone has their own unique way of going about it.

So how do you resolve a situation when everyone's looking after their own interests? You can start by recognizing the different ways people approach a single situation. Do you fight? Clam up? Mediate? Concede? Run?

The ladies of Peerbaugh Place reveal slices of ourselves. Which one are you? As Mae says, "Take your corners, sisters!"

*The Sister Circle:* Chapter 6, page 127

"You can't have people over, *I'm* having people over," [Tessa said.]

"When did this happen?" Mae asked.

"This afternoon while I was at class. We were discussing Elizabethan history and how Walsingham—"

"Walsing-who?"

Tessa's back straightened. "Sir Francis Walsingham. He was the secretary of state to Queen Elizabeth I and developed a secret service of sorts that purged the queen of her enemies. Quite ruthless but very loyal."

"Sounds like a fun guy."

Tessa pursed her lips. "He's an interesting man. Which is why I have three friends coming over at seven to continue our discussion." She nodded toward the batter. "I'm making fruit meringues."

Summer spoke over her shoulder. "We don't get any."

Tessa flashed the little girl a look that surprised Evelyn. But Summer took it well by turning back to her work.

"Well," Mae said, "everyone can have as much of my food offering as they want." She moved to the sink to wash the celery.

Tessa had not moved and the spatula threatened to drip into her hand. "But you don't understand. This is not acceptable. We can't both have people over at the same time."

"Afraid we'll corrupt your discussion, Tessie? Bring in some of the rebellious Irish influence from my Fitzpatrick name?"

Evelyn tensed as Tessa did a quarter turn in her direction. "What are *you* going to do about this *situation*?"

Mae did her own quarter turn, but

added a smile. "Yes, Evelyn, what *are* you going to do about this *situation*?"

"I...I don't really know what—"

Audra came through the door just then, her eyes seeking her daughter. "Hey, baby. Did you have a good day?"

"It was great, Mommy. We cooked and cleaned and—"

Evelyn was glad to change the subject. "How was work?"

Audra hugged Summer from behind. "Oh, it was—"

"Excuse me?" Tessa said. "We have a crisis here."

Audra scanned their faces. "What's going on?"

Mae did the honors. "It seems Tessie and I are engaged in a battle for the parlor. She's invited three of her snooty scholar types over to discuss dead people, and I've invited three of my fabulously amiable friends over to play cards, and—"

Audra put a hand to her mouth. "And I've invited Gillie and Piper over to watch a movie."

"This—" Tessa punctuated the air with the spatula once, spraying a blob of meringue onto the floor. Her hand returned to its place beneath it. "This will not do."

Evelyn wanted to flee. "Oh dear."

Mae stepped into the middle of the kitchen, her hands raised. "Take your corners, sisters. We *will* work this out."

*"Be nice to people on your way up because you'll meet them on your way down."*

Wilson Mizner

"I don't see how."

Mae pointed a finger at Tessa. "Would you and your group be comfortable in the sunroom?"

Tessa glanced toward the room at the back of the house off the kitchen. It was clearly not her first choice. "I was hoping for the parlor. After all, that *is* the most elegant—"

"I won't argue with you there. But my friends and I need a table. If we use the dining room and Audra and her bunch watch a movie in the parlor where the VCR is located…" Mae dropped her chin and challenged Tessa. "Unless you and your friends wouldn't mind the sounds of a hearty card game rising from the next room?"

Tessa opened her mouth, then shut it, then opened it again. "You're not giving me much choice."

Mae shrugged. "Yeah, well…"

Tessa shuffled her shoulders. "I want a choice."

Mae dropped her jaw. "You…? You have a choice. You can either join our card game in the dining room or watch a movie in the parlor. Or you can have your meeting in the relative quiet of the sunroom. Take your pick."

Tessa's eyes flashed. "What happened to the democracy of Peerbaugh Place? Since when does one tenant get to dictate—"

"But you want to dictate—"

Tessa looked surprised. "Me?"

Mae took a step toward Tessa, brandishing a celery stalk. "Who has proclaimed herself the dictator of this house from the first moment she—?"

"I did no such—"

Audra moved between them. "Ladies!"

Mae lowered the celery. "She always has to have her way."

"Only because my way is the best way."

Mae's snicker was thick with contempt. "Our own little Napolèan. How did we get so lucky?"

"Technically, Napolèan was not a dictator. He was an emperor and—"

Mae raised her arms in a mock bow. "Oh, Empress Tessie, how may we serve you?"

Audra pulled one of Mae's hands down. "Come on, you two. We can work this out."

"Not me," Mae said. She suddenly took a musketeer stance with the celery as her sword. "I say *en garde*!"

When Tessa picked up a spoon, Evelyn fled the room. This was ridiculous. She headed to the solace of the front porch. When no one followed to offer their apologies, her anger grew. They were completely missing the point. It didn't matter who used what room—the point was that not one of them had even asked permission to use *any* room. After all, it was her house.

She looked toward the kitchen where loud voices could still be heard.

At least it used to be her house.

*"The reason the way of the transgressor is so hard is because it's so crowded."*

Kin Hubbard

How
wonderful
it is, how
pleasant, when
brothers live
together in
harmony!

## D My iscovery

Which resident of Peerbaugh Place are you rooting for?

_____
_____
_____
_____
_____
_____
_____
_____
_____

## Sister Talk

Learning to resolve conflict requires an understanding of why we do what we do. Until we understand, we aren't going to surrender that area of our life to the Lord so He can make any changes.

Here are four methods of dealing with conflict:

**Avoid (Evelyn):** Deny and ignore, fail to address, pretend nothing ever happened.

**Consequences:** Things never get resolved. You become a teakettle ready to boil over. Until things are resolved you can't move on. You create a pretend world where nothing is wrong. You seek escape.

**Attack (Tessa):** There are five ways to attack:

- Verbal (harsh accusations, demeaning, belittling comments; comparisons; sarcasm; or giving the silent treatment).

- Emotional (withdrawal of affection).

- Physical (abuse, withdrawal of touch).

- Financial (taking control of finances—withholding it or spending it foolishly on yourself or others).

- Spiritual (guilt-trip manipulation).

**Consequences:** Nobody wins because nothing is resolved and feelings are hurt. Distance is created between the Attacker and the victim.

**Adjust (Audra):** Compromises or makes necessary changes to accommodate the other persons opinion. This method requires maturity and stability from all involved. That is probably why adjusting seldom is the first line of defense in dealing with conflict.

**Consequences:** Everyone feels an equal investment in the resolution, therefore a level of contentment is achieved.

**Accept (Mae):** Some things just don't matter. Remember the Rick Warren quote "It's not about you."? Well sometimes it's easy to handle conflict by "accepting" because it

*I am leaving you with a gift—peace of mind and heart. And the peace I give isn't like the peace the world gives. So don't be troubled or afraid.*

really doesn't matter. The danger comes when the acceptance is not genuine or sincere because the repressed feelings will eventually surface and may be more difficult to deal with than the original conflict.

**Consequences:** This is definitely one of those "good news, bad news" scenarios. The good news is – when it really doesn't matter – great! It's over. The bad news is, when it does matter – it's just a matter of time before the whole thing resurfaces.

## My Discovery
How do I handle conflict? What could I do to resolve conflicts faster?

_____

_____

_____

_____

_____

_____

_____

_____

_____

_____

**Sister Talk** As we've seen, dealing with conflict is a reality of life and is influenced by your personality. The magnitude of the conflict is not important. But the method of resolving it has lasting impact on our relationship with others.

And we're not just talking about the big battles. The simple gesture of rushing ahead of someone in the grocery line or giving a curt response to a co-worker has consequences. Through trial and error we create a pattern of behavior that works for us. Right or wrong. Many of us have edged and hedged and wedged our whole lives, dealing with conflict—or trying to avoid it.

Take Tessa. If you are a **Wind/Teacher** personality, conflict is going to blow your way quite often. You can be an unwelcome intruder and disrupt others. You think you are so "right" (you usually are) but like a roaring wind you seldom have tact. The **Wind/Teacher** is more concerned about communicating who you are and what you know, than how you will be received. The satisfaction you get when someone applies the knowledge you have provided is your reward. The trouble is, your confidence in your own view alienates others who might otherwise move to your way of thinking.

Matthew 5:9

God blesses those who work for peace, for they will be called the children of God.

Proverbs 17:1

A dry crust
eaten in peace
is better than
a great feast
with strife.

**D**My **iscovery** Thinking of a situation that worked well, and one that didn't...why did each turn out the way it did? How could I have changed my response to make it turn out better?

_____

_____

_____

_____

_____

_____

_____

_____

_____

_____

_____

How can my sisters help me deal with conflict?

_____

_____

_____

_____

_____

_____

_____

_____

_____

_____

_____

## His Imprint

When you recognize your strengths and weaknesses in dealing with conflict, submit your weaknesses to Christ. Your perspective can be changed and your resolution method influenced by Him. He has promised to give you *His* mind.

Vonette here: Praying with someone is certain to make you feel closer. Bill and I had a long distance courtship with frequent phone calls. Bill initiated our praying together to end our phone dates so it was quite natural for us to continue to pray together after marriage. We begin and end each day by praying together. It is impossible to sincerely pray together when there is unresolved conflict. Whatever issues we face are discussed and prayed about. We have committed to seek God's will, not what Bill wants and not what I want, but what God wants. This allows us to trust God together, go to bed in love and harmony, and awaken the same way. Prayer has kept our relationship an adventure, with minimal conflict and a delight to both of us for more than fifty-four years. The same principle can work with a friend.

impression six
# Forgiveness

> *"Forgiveness is the fragrance
> that the flower leaves on the heel of the
> one who crushed it."*
> *Mark Twain*

*The Sister Circle:* Chapter 12, page 300

There was a crash of dishes and a yelp from Summer. Evelyn bolted from the room. Within seconds the other three bedroom doors flew open, their occupants in the hall.

Summer was on the stairs, frantically gathering the fallen dishes. She looked up at her audience, her face stricken. "I tripped."

"I'll get a towel," Tessa said. She slipped into the bathroom.

Audra rushed down to her and righted a glass that had contained orange juice, while Summer frantically plucked up the Cheerios that were strewn over multiple steps. Milk dripped from the second step onto the third. Evelyn tried not to think of the stain on her carpet runner.

"Here." Tessa returned with two towels, one dry and one damp.

"What were you doing, baby?" Audra said. "You know better than to bring food upstairs. You know that's against the rules. You tell Aunt Evelyn you're sorry for making a mess on her pretty carpet. You—"

Evelyn saw tears in Summer's eyes. "I don't need an apology. It's okay, sweetie."

"It is not okay. She had no right bringing that big tray up those stairs." Audra clucked Summer under the chin. "What were you thinking?"

"But Mommy . . ."

"Mommy nothing. You have got to be more responsible and follow the—"

"Hey, Audra," Mae said. "Lay off. Can't you see what she was doing?"

Audra pressed a towel onto a puddle of milk. "Making a mess, that's what she was doing."

Suddenly, Summer sat on a step, her cupped hand holding fallen Cheerios. Her shoulders sagged and her chin quivered.

Audra flipped a hand. "Don't stop now, little girl. We've still got a lot of mess to clean—"

"Happy Mother's Day, Mommy."

They all froze as the truth blared.

Summer raised her face to her mother. "I was bringing you breakfast in bed. I didn't mean—"

With an expulsion of regret, Audra sidestepped the mess to get to her daughter, pulling her into her arms. "Oh, baby. I'm so sorry, so sorry. I didn't understand."

"I didn't mean to fall."

"Of course you didn't."

"What a good girl," Evelyn said.

"You were trying to carry a bowl of cereal and a glass of juice up here, all by yourself?" Tessa asked.

Summer nodded.

Mae rushed to the top of the landing, taking control. "What can be broken can be fixed." She walked down to their step and held out her hand. "Summer, you come with me."

Summer took her hand warily. "Where we going?"

"To make your mom breakfast in bed."

"But Mommy's up."

Mae flashed Audra a look. "She won't be next time you see her, will she?"

Audra stood. She yawned, stretched, and headed back to her room. "I'm tired. I think I'll go back to bed."

"I thought you looked a little pale." Mae led Summer down the stairs.

Summer remembered the stash of Cheerios in her fist. "What about these?"

"Bring 'em along. Slightly used Cheerios taste the best."

As Mae and Summer disappeared to the kitchen, Evelyn and Tessa fell upon the mess. Audra peeked out from her room. "Need some help?"

Tessa shooed her away. "Get back in there and play your part when she comes back." She pointed with the towel. "You have a gem of a little lady in that girl. I hope you know that."

"I do. I know that."

"Then git."

Audra's door closed.

**Sister Talk** Poor little girl. *Snow/Servers* like Summer crave appreciation for their hard work, buy they don't always get it. Summer had every reason to feel hurt, and yet she also had a choice about how to react: with anger or with quiet acceptance. Her young innocence allowed her to forgive her mother's thoughtlessness. However, when we get older, forgiving can be a strain.

Any time we do something nice for another person, we risk rejection and put ourselves in the position of dealing with the issue of forgiveness. Like the Mary and Martha story in the Bible when Martha gets after her sister Mary for not helping get dinner ready. Mary is talking with Jesus while Martha's busy in the kitchen (and it upset Martha.) Though Martha's desire to serve is very good, we all need to learn to ease up and follow Jesus' advice to Martha: "But the Lord said to her, 'My dear Martha, you are so upset over all these details! There is really only one thing worth being concerned about. Mary has discovered it—and I won't take it away from her.'" (Luke 10: 41-42).

When we serve, we must do it gladly, but be careful not to let it get in the way of more important opportunities. And we need to forgive those who don't give us enough pats on the back. Do it for Him, not them.

# $D^{My}_{iscovery}$ Name a time I felt unappreciated. How did I react? How did others react to my reaction? What could I have done to make the situation better?

_____

_____

_____

_____

_____

_____

_____

_____

_____

_____

_____

_____

_____

_____

_____

_____

_____

_____

_____

_____

_____

**Sister Talk** The need—the opportunity—to forgive can come to us daily. From the small stuff like your husband not getting gas in the car when he'd promised, to the larger issue of a friend sharing a confidence she'd promised to keep secret. You are called—by God—to forgive. Not just once, but as many times as it takes. It's not a suggestion. It's a direct instruction from Jesus to all of us.

Peter asked the question in Matthew 18: 21-22:

"Then Peter came to him and asked, 'Lord, how often should I forgive someone who sins against me? Seven times?'

'No!' Jesus replied, 'seventy times seven!' "

Seventy times seven . . . four hundred and ninety times! I guess we'd probably be safe at 491, but by the time we got that far, wouldn't we be willing to forgive one more time? That's the blessing of forgiveness. It benefits you, the forgiver, just as much (if not more) than the one who's being forgiven. It softens your heart. It draws you closer to God. It makes you a better woman.

Note that you're not being asked to forget. Just to forgive. But again, as you open yourself to this act of love, you *will* let the past go. You will forget, at least enough to look forward instead of back.

"There is one eternal principle which will be valid as long as the world lasts. The principle is: forgiveness is a costly thing ..."
William Barclay

# $D_{iscovery}^{My}$ Who do I need to forgive?

_____

_____

_____

_____

_____

_____

_____

_____

## Should I be ashamed of some action?

_____

_____

_____

_____

_____

_____

_____

_____

_____

How can I forget about the incident?

**Sister Talk** The issue of forgiveness always includes an element of guilt and/or shame. Whether we feel shame for something we've done, or we feel guilty for not forgiving someone else's act against us, if we don't deal with the forgiveness it can become an oozing wound. And a Band-Aid won't fix it. Besides, as Karen Brown says in her delightful book, *The Joy of Sisters*, "A savvy sis knows that the one who apologizes always gets the last word."

It's not always easy. As women, we often keep tabs on faults and mistakes—whether they're our own, or someone else's. We're very hard on ourselves and each other. Yet healing starts with forgiving ourselves. If you can't forgive yourself for the mistakes you've made, how can you genuinely forgive other people? How can you extend what you don't have?

There are consequences to not forgiving. An unforgiving spirit breeds bitterness, and a bitter woman is not capable of living the life God designed for her. Is this God's fault? Too many times God is blamed. If you play the blame-game you are not accepting the beautiful life that Christ's death on the cross provided.

> "The weak can never forgive. Forgiveness is the attribute of the strong."
>
> Mahatma Gandhi

# My Discovery

What steps can I take to relieve these feelings of guilt?

_____
_____
_____
_____
_____
_____
_____
_____
_____
_____
_____
_____
_____
_____
_____
_____
_____
_____
_____
_____
_____
_____

_____

_____

_____

_____

_____

_____

_____

_____

**Sister Talk** The joy and release that comes when you can forgive yourself is divine—truly "Capital-D" Divine. Forgiving yourself is loving yourself. You are commanded to love others as you love yourself (which assumes you *do* love yourself!)

> *You must love them as you love yourself.*
>
> Leviticus 19: 34

> *We love each other as a result of*
> ***HIS*** *loving us first.*
> 1 John 4: 19

When a woman truly understands who she is in Christ, she has a forgiving spirit. Being in her presence encourages both of you to flourish in your spiritual development.

*Get rid of all bitterness, rage, anger, harsh words,*
*and slander, as well as all types of malicious behavior.*
*Instead, be kind to each other, tenderhearted, forgiving one another, just as God through Christ has forgiven you.*

Ephesians 4: 31-32

Forgiving is a necessity of life. It's our duty and our privilege. Does the person we need to forgive deserve it? Do we? Probably not, but that doesn't matter. After all, Christ died on the cross to forgive all of ours sins, past, present, and future. He, who had *never* sinned, died for us! Isn't that amazing? And humbling?

Here's the bottom line: "If you forgive those who sin against you, your heavenly Father will forgive you. But if you refuse to forgive others, your Father will not forgive your sins" (Matthew 6: 14-15). Can't get much plainer than that.

## My Discovery

How can my sisters help me forgive or be forgiven?

_____

_____

_____

_____

_____

"Forgiveness is the answer to the child's dream of a miracle by which what is broken is made whole again, what is soiled is again made clean."

Dag Hammarskjold

## His Imprint

As we've worked through the Impression on forgiveness, we realize that some of you may need to rethink your understanding of God's forgiveness of your sin nature. If you can't accept His forgiveness of you, forgiving yourself and forgiving others will be impossible. Can you pray this simple prayer?

"Father, Thank you for loving me when I haven't loved myself. I accept your forgiveness."

*God the Father chose you long ago, and the Spirit has made you holy.*
*As a result, you have obeyed Jesus Christ and are cleansed by his blood.*
*May you have more and more of God's special favor and wonderful peace.*

1 Peter 1:2

impression seven
# Confidence

*Surely your goodness and unfailing love*
*will pursue me all the days of my life,*
*and I will live in the house of the Lord forever.*

Psalm 23:6

*The Sister Circle:* Chapter 10, page 260

In a single movement Piper tossed her keys on her kitchen counter and shucked off her shoes. Then she confronted her empty apartment. One more evening, alone.

Although Evelyn had invited her to spend the evening with her and Tessa, Piper had declined. On the way home she'd justified it to herself by pointing out that it wasn't normal for a thirty-three-year-old woman to spend an evening with two much older women. It sounded good as excuses went.

The truth was, Piper hadn't wanted to spend the evening with Evelyn and Tessa because she wanted to feel sorry for herself, and that was hard to do in the presence of good company. Plus, jealousy came into play. Audra had a boyfriend; Mae had a boyfriend; Evelyn was venturing out of her widowhood by taking a cooking class, and Tessa ... skip Tessa. The lives of the ladies of Peerbaugh Place were turning into a Disneyland compared to her county fair.

So God has given us both his promise and his oath. These two things are unchangeable because it is impossible for God to lie. Therefore, we who have fled to him for refuge can take new courage, for we can hold on to his promise with confidence.

Her life wasn't bad, but it was so ... so *known*. One day flowing into another. Work, home, work, home. With an occasional excursion out with a friend. But even that was difficult because most of her friends were married with children. She trudged through life as an odd number. A three in a group of two. A fifth at a table for four.

*Why doesn't anything exciting ever happen to me?*

**Sister Talk** Do you feel like Piper? Is your feeling justified? Could you be doing exactly what you're supposed to be doing but you've merely hit a wall of discouragement? It's important to identify the truth behind these moments of doubt because one answer should lead you toward an important change in your life, while another answer should lead you toward finding contentment. Know yourself. Accept doubt as part of life, but deal with it. Use it. Be wise about it.

If you're like Piper, a **Sunshine/Perceiver,** you are very intuitive and sensitive to God's call— even if you don't understand it. Piper was single and she didn't want to be. And yet, she also realized God had a plan playing out within her situation—just as He has a plan for you within your life situation. The challenge is to open yourself to find out what that plan is.

The **Sunshine/Perceiver** understands. You illuminate your world with a boldness that can clarify life. You frequently closet yourself for fear of being misunderstood because you see and understand what others don't. The **Sunshine/Perceiver** doesn't just see the good , but also the bad, and this fact forces you to tap into your courage in order to confront. Confrontation can provoke and yet insight is needed to shed light on the world.

As with all the spiritual gifts and personality types, there is a bit of the shining **Sunshine/ Perceiver** in all of us. Let's tap into that. Being a good perceiver leads to a purposeful future.

D**My** **iscovery** In what ways am I good at understanding situations, sensing things about people, using my women's intuition?

_____

_____

_____

_____

_____

_____

_____

*This confidence is like a strong and trustworthy anchor for our souls. It leads us through the curtain of heaven into God's inner sanctuary.*

97

Isaiah 30:15

"Only in returning to Me and waiting for me will you be saved. In quietness and confidence is your strength."

**Sister Talk** At this point in the *Diary* we're asking you to be bold, to set aside the woman you've been, and think of yourself in a new, exciting way—God's way. Often when we start gaining confidence in our purpose—by even taking the simple step of admitting we *have* a unique purpose—our attitude changes. We change. Like Evelyn (in Chapter 3 of *The Sister Circle*). It's as if the door of the cage has been thrown open and we're able to fly.

But it's scary to fly when we've lived in a contained space, with a defined, known plan. Most of us go many, many years without even realizing our real purpose *might* be out *there*, away from where we *are*.

Perhaps we've been sampling our real purpose for years, and have even become accustomed to its slightly bland taste, thinking what we were doing was as good as it gets. But know this: there's *more*. When we let God season our purpose with His salt, it—and we—come alive and there's no going back. Ever. Then it grows. Once our taste buds have been whetted with this new seasoning of life, we crave more, and more, and get more adventurous in trying something new. With God empowering us, our lives become a feast of purpose—a banquet of opportunities.

**D**My **iscovery**  Read these next verses carefully; read them aloud. Apply them to yourself.  In fact, we've taken out the word "you" and "your" so you can insert your name in the blanks:

"_____ is the salt of the earth. But what good is salt if it has lost its flavor?

Can _____ make it useful again?

It will be thrown out and trampled underfoot as worthless.

_____ is the light of the world—like a city on a mountain, glowing in the night for all to see.

Don't hide _____'s light under a basket!

Instead, put it on a stand and let it shine for all.

In the same way, let _____'s good deeds shine out for all to see,

so that everyone will praise _____'s heavenly Father."

*Matthew 5: 13-16*

## Sister Talk

That's pretty powerful, isn't it? The verses almost become a prayer . . . In fact, say it again. Pray it again.

God is telling *YOU* to spice up the world; not blend in, but season it, bring out the best in it. And our God-given gifts do no good hidden under a basket. Let them out! Let them shine! For His glory! We dare not lose our flavor or dull our light! Too much is at stake.

## My Discovery

What is my light?

_____

_____

_____

_____

_____

_____

_____

_____

_____

_____

_____

_____

_____

*Philippians 3:3*

We put no confidence in human effort. Instead, we boast about what Christ Jesus has done for us.

The LORD will work out His plans for my life—for Your faithful love, O LORD, endures forever. Don't abandon me, for You made me.

How would my sisters describe my light?

_____

_____

_____

_____

_____

_____

_____

_____

_____

What "baskets" cover my "light" from the world, dulling my light—and God's? Is my basket made of fear, false humility, timidity, hesitancy, procrastination, panic, selfishness?

_____

_____

_____

_____

_____

_____

_____

_____

_____

How can I remove my basket?

For fun . . . if I were a seasoning sprinkled on the world, I would be—Salt? Cayenne pepper? Paprika? Basil?

Does my purpose involve mellowing out
the flavor of the world?  Or spicing it up?

_____

_____

_____

_____

_____

_____

_____

_____

_____

_____

_____

**Sister Talk**  As you have journeyed through the
pages of your *Discovery Diary* you have
been asked to admit some telling truths.  We hope
you recognize the most exciting truth of all:  that
God loves you and is eager to see you develop the
gifts He has given you. Boldness develops when
we begin to see evidence that the abilities He
has given us are truly being applied and are
beneficial.  Let us be bold!

Part of loving ourselves and becoming
all we can be is allowing other people to

become all they can be and loving them for who they are. We need to take every opportunity to encourage others. Verbally recognize the mom with a well-behaved child in a grocery store, the friendly teller at the bank, or (perhaps the hardest of all) say something nice to that guy you live with. Notice when his socks match his pants, or when the mowed lawn looks like velvet. Appreciate people for who they are. We need to have confidence that God didn't make a mistake in creating *any* of us. And through that self-confidence, confidence based on Him, we can fulfill God's purpose, be bold, and achieve our dreams. So don't waste another moment wandering down the wrong road.

*Show me the path where I should walk, O LORD;*
*point out the right road for me to follow.*
*Lead me by your truth and teach me,*
*for you are the God who saves me. All day long I*
*put my hope in you.*

Psalm 25: 4-5

One more thing . . . as we near the end of this *Discovery Diary*, let's dispel one myth, one copout. Too many times we complain that it's someone else's fault we aren't all we can be. NO ONE else can make our life productive and rooted in our purpose. They may contribute or hinder, but they are not totally responsible. We cannot control other people. We can only control ourselves, and in turn let our lives be God-controlled. We smile at the adage, "The devil made me do it" but let's live the adage, "God made me do it. God *enabled* me to do it."

## $\mathcal{D}^{\text{My}}_{\text{iscovery}}$  Who (or what) have I been blaming for not being all I can be?

_____

_____

_____

_____

_____

_____

_____

_____

_____

_____

_____

_____

_____

How can I change that attitude?

_____

_____

_____

_____

_____

_____

_____

_____

_____

_____

_____

_____

_____

_____

_____

**Sister Talk** There's a story about a woman who stands before God and asks Him a question: "There's so much sadness and evil in the world; there's so much to be done. Why don't you send someone?" To which God replied, "I did. I sent you."

Did you feel chills at that punchline? Grab onto those words. Cherish them. And be challenged by them, because it's true. HE SENT YOU!

Which leads us to the climax of this *Discovery Diary*. The very last thing we want you to write down is not who you are, what fault you want to correct, but *who do you want to become*?

D**My**iscovery Recognizing that it is constantly evolving, what is my God-given purpose?

_____

_____

_____

_____

_____

_____

_____

_____

_____

_____

_____

_____

_____

Describe the woman I want to be.

_____
_____
_____
_____
_____
_____
_____
_____
_____
_____
_____
_____
_____
_____
_____
_____
_____
_____
_____

Who can be my role model?

_____
_____
_____

What can I do—TODAY—toward
becoming that woman?

_____
_____
_____
_____
_____

Is there a sister who can help me in my pursuit?

_____
_____
_____
_____
_____

## His Imprint

The greatest joy for a Christian woman is to live
life knowing she is loved by her Creator, designed
with a purpose, and living out that purpose.

*How can we understand the road we travel?*
*It is the LORD who directs our steps.*

Proverbs 20: 24

# To Be a REAL Sister:

Remember the Sister Circle pledge: we are to encourage each other with outbursts of love and good deeds. So do it. Enjoy each others' dreams, revel in our unique purposes, and help each other accomplish our personal goals!

# Sister Circle Prayer:

*Heavenly Father, thank you for bringing us through this journey of discovery. We commit our lives to You and by Your grace we will live with passion and purpose. Bind us together in sisterhood, and help us to love ourselves and each other as You love us.*

# Note from Nancy and Vonette:

We hope you sense the faith and confidence we have in you. May all your discoveries delight and reflect His glory!

*Nancy and Vonette*